Malcolm X

Malcolm X

by Arnold Adoff
illustrated by John Wilson

 HarperCollins*Publishers*

MALCOLM X
Text copyright © 1970 by Arnold Adoff
Illustrations copyright © 1970 John Wilson
All rights reserved. No part of this book may be used or reproduced
in any manner whatsoever without written permission except in the
case of brief quotations embodied in critical articles and reviews.
Printed in the United States of America. For information address
HarperCollins Children's Books, a division of HarperCollins Publishers,
10 East 53rd Street, New York, NY 10022.

Library of Congress Catalog Card Number 70-94787
ISBN 0-690-51413-1
ISBN 0-690-51414-X (lib. bdg.)

7   8   9   10

Malcolm X

The house was quiet. Louisa Little sat very still, listening. She could hear the sound of horses galloping closer and closer.

Maybe the horses would gallop by her house. Maybe, if she stayed very quiet, the house would seem empty.

One by one Louisa's three children came and huddled around her. Then there was silence. Louisa glanced out the window. She saw burning and smoking torches. They were held high by men who wore white hoods over their heads and white sheets over their clothing. They looked like ghosts in the eerie light of their flaming sticks.

Louisa Little was frightened. Her husband, Reverend Earl Little, was away at a meeting. She didn't know when he would return home. The men outside were Klansmen. She could see their shotguns and rifles. She knew they hated her and her children because the Littles were black.

Klansmen belonged to a group of white people called the Ku Klux Klan. They rode the countryside frightening black people. Sometimes they shot and killed black people for no reason at all. The Klan simply hated. The Klan wanted to keep black people poor and afraid.

But Reverend Little wasn't afraid to speak out against the Klansmen. In the Baptist churches where he was the minister, he told the black people that they had a right to good jobs and good homes. He told them that they were as good as any white people.

Now the Klansmen rode around Reverend Little's house trying to scare him into silence.

Suddenly the butt of a gun shattered a window. The glass fell into the room where Mrs. Little and her children tried to hide. Then came the noise of a window crashing in on the other side of the house. The Klansmen smashed every window in the house that night. Then they rode away. When Reverend Little returned home, he found that his

wife and children were safe. But there was broken glass all around them. He was glad they had not been hurt.

Soon afterward, on May 19, 1925, a fourth child was born to the Littles. The child was a boy, with light brown skin and reddish hair. The Littles named him Malcolm. While he was still a baby, the family moved from their house in Omaha, Nebraska, to Lansing, Michigan.

But trouble followed Reverend Little. In Michigan he went right on preaching that all men were equal. He told black people not to let white people treat them like servants. White men tried again to silence him. They set fire to the house he had found for his family and ran away when Reverend Little shot at them. The house burned to the ground because the firemen and police just stood around and watched.

Again the Littles had to move. They went far out into the country. They built a nice four-room house and hoped that this time they would be safe.

A few years later Reverend Little was killed. A streetcar ran over him. Friends whispered that the reverend's death had been no accident. Malcolm also believed that white men had killed his father and then placed his body on the tracks.

After her husband's death Mrs. Little was left with very little money. She would stand over the stove and try to make vegetables and stale bread into a decent meal. Malcolm stayed so hungry, he was often weak.

Sometimes he and his brothers went hunting in the woods. When they were lucky, they caught a rabbit, which they took home for supper. Mrs. Little worked hard to hold her family together. Malcolm's oldest brother, Wilfred, quit school

and tried to help her with the children. But Mrs.
Little was always so worried and tired that she
became ill.

The state welfare workers were often at the
house. They thought the children should go live
with other families. They called Mrs. Little
"crazy." Finally she was sent to the State Hospital
at Kalamazoo.

Malcolm was only twelve years old when his

mother was taken away from him. He and his brothers and sisters moved in with other families in Lansing. But Malcolm soon got into trouble without a mother or father to watch out for him. He was placed in a detention home.

The detention home was run by a white man and woman. They were kind and liked Malcolm but they did not think that black people were as good as white. They never seemed to notice that what they said hurt Malcolm's feelings.

Malcolm's father had taught him that he was as important as anybody else. He didn't understand why the white couple talked about black people as though they were animals.

Malcolm was one of the smartest students in his school. In the seventh grade, he was elected president of his class. He felt proud of himself. He was on the basketball team, too. He began to dream of growing up and becoming an educated

man. His English teacher, Mr. Ostrowski, asked Malcolm about his future plans. And Malcolm said he wanted to become a lawyer. Mr. Ostrowski looked surprised when he heard Malcolm's dream. He had never heard of a black boy wanting to be a lawyer.

Black boys didn't become lawyers, Mr. Ostrowski told Malcolm. Perhaps he could make things with his hands, instead. Yes, many black men became carpenters. Why couldn't Malcolm do that?

Malcolm was hurt. Once more someone had told him that he was inferior. Slowly, he began to change inside. He drew away from the white boys and girls. He could hardly sit through English class because he knew Mr. Ostrowski didn't respect him. He wondered if being a black boy was something to be ashamed of. Sad and alone,

Malcolm began to feel less proud of himself.

After finishing the eighth grade in school, Malcolm was released from the detention home. He boarded a Greyhound bus and traveled to Boston to live with his sister Ella. He never went back to school again. Instead he became a shoe-shine boy in a dance hall. He started selling "reefers," or marijuana cigarettes, and illegal liquor. He learned to drink and gamble and he himself smoked marijuana. Malcolm had to be careful of the police, for he was now in danger of being arrested.

Next, Malcolm sold sandwiches on the train between Boston and New York. That was how he found his way to Harlem, the neighborhood in New York City where many thousands of black people live.

Harlem became home to Malcolm. He loved it

from the moment he saw all the black people there. And he never stopped loving it.

Malcolm found a job as a waiter at Small's Paradise, a restaurant and nightclub. At Small's Malcolm met the people of Harlem. He met cooks, waiters, bartenders, laborers, teachers, and even criminals. Malcolm liked everybody and everybody liked him. Now he was over six feet tall and good-looking, with freckles. He still had reddish hair, and people began to call him "Big Red." Malcolm felt as though he had lived in Harlem all his life.

Malcolm talked often to the men who were criminals. Perhaps he was taken by their flashy clothes and fancy cars. They always had money in their pockets. They always had time to teach Malcolm "hustles"—ways to make money dishonestly.

It was not long before Malcolm became a

young hustler himself. He started to sell reefers again. He worked for the white gangsters who bossed the crime in Harlem. Whenever he knew the police were looking for him, he took the train to Boston. He stayed in his sister's house until it was safe to come back.

In Boston Malcolm teamed up with an old pal from Lansing and two girls he'd met. The team broke into houses at night and stole clothing,

jewelry, and whatever else they could find. Finally Malcolm was caught by the police and sent to the Charlestown State Prison in Massachusetts. He was twenty years old.

At Charlestown Malcolm was miserable. The prison was very old and dingy. There was no running water in the cells. Malcolm could stretch his arms out and touch the walls—his cell was that small. His toilet was a covered pail in one corner.

The judge had given him a ten-year sentence in jail. The usual sentence for a first arrest was only two years. Malcolm grew angry whenever he thought of the judge.

The other prisoners called Malcolm "Satan." He acted mean. He was always getting into trouble. He threw things out of his cell and dis-obeyed orders at meals. Malcolm was often placed in "solitary," a cell by himself.

Three years later, Malcolm was transferred to Norfolk Prison Colony. It was a newer, better-run prison, with a fine library. Malcolm had not read books since the eighth grade. But now he began to take them out of the prison library. These books were to change his life.

It was difficult for Malcolm to understand many of the words he read, so he got a dictionary. From it he copied page after page into notebooks.

This is how he learned the meanings of many new words. Malcolm also discovered famous people and places listed in the dictionary. It was like studying a small encyclopedia.

Reading and learning became all that Malcolm cared about in prison. He often read books for fifteen hours a day. Even after the lights were turned out in his cell, Malcolm read until three and four o'clock in the morning by the glow of the light in the corridor. He strained his eyes so badly that he had to wear glasses.

Malcolm read most about the life of the black man in Africa and America. He read that black people had great societies in Africa long before America was discovered. He learned about the kingdoms of Benin, Ghana, and Ethiopia, which began more than five hundred years before the birth of Jesus.

In his history book in junior high school, Malcolm had found only one paragraph about black Americans. Now he read books by and about black people. He read about Frederick Douglass, who had been a slave and became a great speaker and leader of his people. He read books by W. E. B. Du Bois, a teacher and writer who had started the National Association for the Advancement of Colored People. Malcolm had never known about these men before.

During his years in prison Malcolm wrote letters to his brothers and sisters. His brother Reginald often came from Detroit to visit him. Reginald talked with pride about a new religion he had joined. It was called the Nation of Islam. Its followers, who were sometimes called "Black Muslims," practiced the Muslim religion.

The Muslims believed that black people should be as respected as white people. They wanted black people to live in separate communities like Harlem. They wanted them to own their own businesses. In this way, black people would be free from white people.

Reginald told Malcolm about the Nation of Islam and about its leader, the Honorable Elijah Muhammad. Mr. Muhammad lived in Chicago. He called white people "devils" who had always tried to enslave blacks. Malcolm felt from his own experiences and from his reading that Elijah Muhammad told the truth.

Malcolm was excited by what he heard. For the first time since his father's death, he heard a black man telling other black men to be strong and proud.

Malcolm began to write letters to Mr. Muhammad. Mr. Muhammad wrote back. Soon Malcolm was writing every day. He wrote about the

awful feeling he had when he read how black people were sold into slavery. And he wrote about his happiness when he discovered that black people had always fought against slavery in America.

Malcolm became a convert to the Muslim religion. He changed his name from Malcolm Little to Malcolm X. "Little" had been the name of the slave master who had long ago given his own name to Malcolm's ancestors. They had not been called "Little" when they were forced onto the slave ships on the African coast. No black American knows the African name of his ancestors. So the Muslims used the letter "X." It showed that they could never know their true last names.

The Muslims did not like to be called "Negroes." In slavery times the word had been used by slave owners. It was part of the white world.

Instead, Muslims used the words "black" or "Afro-American."

The Nation of Islam was always kind to black people who had gone to jail. It taught them the Muslim religion while they were in prison and helped them find jobs when they got out.

Muslim men dressed neatly in dark suits. The women wore white dresses and covered their heads with scarves. Muslims did not drink alcohol or smoke cigarettes. They were taught that the Muslim family should live together in love and harmony. They practiced their religion in temples, or mosques, similar to churches.

In the summer of 1952 Malcolm X was let out of prison on parole. He was happy to be a free man again. His first stop was a Turkish bath. He wanted the steam and hot water to wash away the dirty prison feeling.

Malcolm decided to go live in Detroit with his brother Wilfred, who was also a Muslim. He hoped to get a fresh start in a town where the police did not know him. In Detroit he worked as a furniture salesman for a while, and then on the assembly line in a factory. He shared the Muslim family life and went to meetings at the Detroit Temple Number One.

In September Malcolm visited Chicago, where

the Nation of Islam had its headquarters. Here, at last, he met the Honorable Elijah Muhammad. At first Malcolm could only stare at this gentle man who had taken the time to write so often to a prisoner. Elijah Muhammad was brown-skinned, small, and soft-spoken. To Malcolm he seemed almost tiny, and fragile. But when Elijah Muhammad talked about the black man's troubles in America, his voice was strong and angry. Right then Malcolm decided he wanted to work for the Nation of Islam.

Mr. Muhammad felt he knew Malcolm from his letters. He liked the honest way Malcolm talked. They had lunch together in Mr. Muhammad's home. Elijah Muhammad thought that Malcolm could become a fine speaker for the Muslims.

In the summer of 1953 Malcolm became an assistant minister in Detroit Temple Number One. Each day he went to the black neighborhoods. He talked to people in restaurants and bars and on street corners, hoping to convert them to the Muslim religion.

Malcolm X worked hard for the next six years. He founded new temples in Philadelphia, New York, and many other cities. He made many speeches. "Stand up for your right to be men," he told his listeners.

Elijah Muhammad became ill. Malcolm X took on more and more of his work. Soon he was known all over the United States as the spokesman for the Nation of Islam.

"I have pledged on my knees to Allah," he would say, "to tell the white man about his crimes and the black man the true teachings of our Honorable Elijah Muhammad."

People began to say that Malcolm might one day take Elijah Muhammad's place. They believed he was a sincere and honest man. When Malcolm said white people had committed crimes against black people, they listened and knew it was true.

Thousands of black people understood what Malcolm said. He had been a convict. He had been hungry and poor. Now he was trying to help all poor black people to live better lives.

The membership of the Nation of Islam grew

to more than forty thousand people. But there were many people who would not join the religion. They believed Malcolm was a black man who hated whites. But Malcolm told all who would listen: "I am not condemning whites for being white but for their deeds."

Malcolm wanted most to teach black Americans one important thing. He taught that blacks must not let white people keep them from living as freely as other Americans.

"All black men are angry," Malcolm would often say, "and I am the angriest black man in America."

Malcolm did get angry when people said he hated all white people. But he tried to control his anger. He never wanted to do anything that would make black people ashamed of him. Malcolm hoped to make black people proud of them-

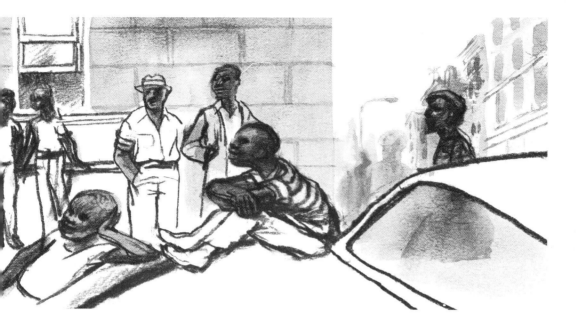

selves and to make a new place for them in America.

Malcolm told the world that the more than twenty million black people in America were the same as prisoners. "If you're born in America with a black skin," he said, "you're born in prison."

Malcolm traveled all over the country. He came often to New York City and he walked through

Harlem. On the crowded side streets and avenues, people gathered around to greet him and shake his hand. Malcolm X was their hero. He spoke easily to them and asked them to give up alcohol and drugs. He joked with them. Even the black people who could not believe in the Muslim religion trusted Malcolm. They knew Malcolm would never lie to them or try to hurt them.

While in New York, Malcolm met a young woman who was a member of the Muslim temple there. Her name was Betty X. After a courtship, Malcolm married Betty in 1958. Over the years Malcolm and his wife had four daughters. The family lived in a house in Queens, New York.

Life for Malcolm was always busy. He worked eighteen hours a day. He was away for weeks at a time on speaking tours. The months and years passed quickly.

Then trouble began with the other leaders in the Nation of Islam. There were long months of unhappy disagreements. Malcolm X started thinking about his place in the Muslim religion. It was a time of great change and growth in him. He wanted to find a way to bring all black Americans together to fight for their rights.

In 1964 Malcolm made two trips to Africa and the Middle East. First he made a pilgrimage to the holy city of Mecca in Saudi Arabia. Mecca was the birthplace of the prophet Muhammad, founder of the Muslim religion. Here Malcolm was treated as a friend by both white and black Muslims. After talking with them, he felt that maybe black and white people in America could work together to end injustice and poverty.

Malcolm took the name of El-Hajj Malik El-Shabazz. The title was an honor. It was given by the Muslims to those who had made the pilgrimage to Mecca.

Malcolm also visited Ghana and Nigeria in West Africa. He met with black leaders of many African nations. He hoped to bring together the black man's struggles in America and in Africa. The black man in Africa was trying to free himself, too.

Life changed for Malcolm X Shabazz. He left the Nation of Islam. In Africa he had seen how

Christian and Muslim black people worked together. Now he wanted to lead a movement in America of black Christians as well as Muslims. Malcolm formed his own group. He called it the Organization of Afro-American Unity.

Some Muslims were angry at Malcolm for leaving the Nation of Islam. And there were whites who did not want black people to unite with Malcolm as their leader. He was often followed by carloads of armed men. In the night, frightening telephone calls disturbed the peace of his home. Unknown voices threatened him with death.

One night a flaming firebomb crashed through his living room window. Fire filled the room as Malcolm quickly led his wife and children to safety. The house was badly damaged and the family's belongings destroyed. But Malcolm went on with his work.

A week later his organization held a meeting in New York. The date was February 21, 1965. People filled the Audubon Ballroom, where Malcolm was to speak. A burst of applause greeted him as he came forward on the stage. When the applause died down, there was sudden, angry shouting. People were pushing and shoving in the front rows.

"Hold it, hold it!" Malcolm ordered. "Don't get excited! Let's cool it, brothers!"

Then came the loud crack of gunfire. Malcolm fell backward onto the floor. He had been shot.

People screamed. Some rushed to Malcolm's side. Others hurried to his wife, Betty. Malcolm was taken to the hospital, where doctors worked frantically to save his life. But it was too late.

Malcolm X was dead. He was only thirty-nine years old.

All over the world people were shocked at the

news of Malcolm's death. Black people felt sick at heart. In Harlem, they gathered in the streets to talk about this man who had made them proud to be black. Malcolm had loved his black brothers and sisters, and they had loved themselves because of him.

Since his death, love for Malcolm has grown until it is so strong that nothing can take it away.

Today Malcolm X is loved every place that black people live. They speak of him fondly, as though he were someone they knew well who lived on the same street.

In a way, Malcolm X does live on the streets where black people live. For whenever you see proud black men and women, you know that Malcolm X has come close to them.

ABOUT THE AUTHOR

When asked about writing his biography of Malcolm X, **Arnold Adoff** said he feels it is very important for young people to know about this fine man. He went on to say, "I followed his career closely, heard and saw him on radio and television, and learned much from his speeches and writing."

Arnold Adoff is an acclaimed poet and anthologist. Among his many awards and honors is the 1988 NCTE Award for Excellence in Poetry for Children, which he received for the body of his work. He's had over thirty books published, including SPORTS PAGES (HarperCollins, 1986). Mr. Adoff lives in Ohio with his wife, distinguished author Virginia Hamilton.

ABOUT THE ILLUSTRATOR

John Wilson's paintings and prints have been exhibited throughout the country. He has received a John Hay Whitney Fellowship, a James William Paige Traveling Fellowship, and several awards at the National Art Exhibit. In recent years Mr. Wilson has concentrated on sculpture, and in 1986 his commemorative statue of Martin Luther King, Jr., was unveiled in the U.S. Capitol in Washington, D.C. Mr. Wilson now lives in Brookline, Massachusetts.

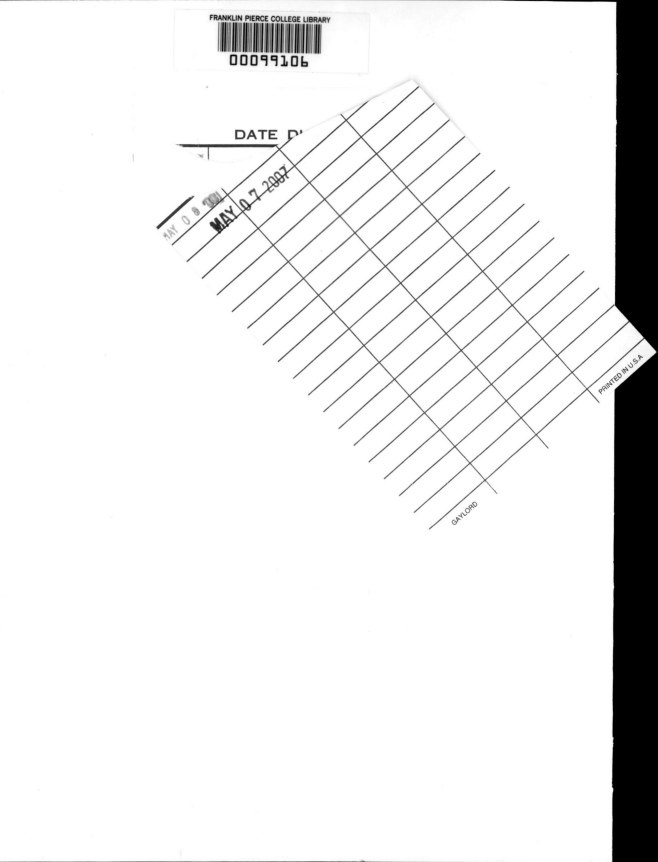